EASY FANTASY 2
CHERRY BLOSSOMS COLORING BOOK

RELAX WITH THE NEW FANTASY COLORING SYSTEM

Fantasy Coloring Books 4

DRAGANA DJ. JEREMIC

dragana.jeremic@relax8.space

https://relax8.space

Independent Publishing

Book design

Dragana Dj. Jeremic

Limits of Liability and Disclaimer of Warranty

The author and publisher shall not be liable for your misuse of this material. This book is strictly for informational and educational purposes.

Warning – Disclaimer

The purpose of this book is to educate and entertain. The author and/or publisher do not guarantee that anyone following these techniques, suggestions, tips, ideas, or strategies will become successful. The author and/or publisher shall have neither liability nor responsibility to anyone with respect to any loss or damage caused, or alleged to be caused, directly or indirectly by the information contained in this book.

INFORMATION AVAILABLE ON THE INTERNET

You may find relevant info at Dragana's Amazon author pages:

US

https://amazon.com/author/draganajoy

UK

https://www.amazon.co.uk/-/e/B07RN2HNBJ

Germany

https://www.amazon.de/-/e/B07RN2HNBJ

France

https://www.amazon.fr/l/B07SN5FHP7?_encoding=UTF8&redirectedFromKindleDbs=true&ref_=pe_1805951_64028601&rfkd=1&shoppingPortalEnabled=true

Also Visit Dragana at:

https://relax8.space/

https://www.facebook.com/dragana.jeremic.5492

Goodreads: https://www.goodreads.com/author/show/19310244.Dragana_Djordje_Jeremic

YOUR PRINTABLE GIFT

Thank you for buying my *Easy Fantasy 2 Cherry Blossoms Coloring Book*. I, Dragana, would like to create an online relationship with you. Let's explore what else is possible.

Your gift is the PDF file with 3 new coloring pages you can enjoy in any space you choose. Each Easy Fantasy Cherry Blossoms coloring page contains 3 flowers that are presented in three versions.

You may discover what is similar to the coloring pages in this book and what is different from them. If you opt-in for this gift you will have a chance to:

- Color three pages that are easy to carry anywhere.

- Relax in the process.

- Be aware of alterations in the coloring pages which will enhance your ability to notice small changes and adapt to them.

Please visit https://relax8.space/variety1/ for the opt-in page that leads to your gift! Keep the link private.

ABOUT THE AUTHOR

Dragana has made her passion to encourage people to relax more.

It is easy to neglect free time, unwinding and the calmness. Many people forget or underestimate relaxation. Are you aware what consequences might be?

To help people appreciate relaxation and integrate it into the daily routine, Dragana Dj. Jeremic offers three paths.

First, we study stress and relaxation.

Second, let us discover how to choose the relaxation techniques and practice them regularly.

Third, you may deal with deeper patterns that block your relaxation advancement.

It is up to you to choose which path is best for you or we may estimate that together during the life coaching sessions. Mail to DJcoach@relax8.space

The author is a lifelong learner and internationally oriented individual. She provides a wider perspective on life challenges. It might be significant Dragana even graduated the University in London with honors in 2003.

Dragana is trained as a psychologist, and autogenic training international instructor.

She has certificates in Life Coaching, Hypnosis, and NLP. In addition, Dragana hold certificates in Ho'oponopono, the Law of Attraction and Values & Ethics in Energy Healing.

SUMMARY OF DETERMINED™ COLORING BOOK

Dragana Dj. Jeremic is glad to inform you about her new fantasy coloring system named DETERMINED coloring book.

First, we have several perspectives. Each perspective is a different visual representation of the main theme. Alternatively, we may deal with only one perspective in an easy approach to fantasy coloring books.

Second, Dragana presents each perspective on three levels based on the number and size of the main elements, here cherry blossoms. We may compare it to an establishing shot, American shot and close up in the film industry.

Third, Dragana adds the fantasy elements to each level. There are three versions of each level. We explore white flowers with fantasy pattern environment. Next, we focus on symbol patterns flowers with natural environment. Final, we pay attention to mandala pattern flowers with natural environment.

THE ELEMENTS OF EASY FANTASY 2

CHERRY BLOSSOMS COLORING BOOK

We have one perspective and three levels. The approach is simple: let's focus on flowers without the environment. On each level we handle white flowers, mandala pattern blossoms and symbol design blooms.

9+1 COLORING PAGES IN 1 PERSPECTIVE

One Perspective: Nine Coloring Pages, 3x3

Level A: 12 Flowers

Level B: 7 Flowers

Level C: 2 Flowers

The Bonus: One Coloring Page of Natural Cherry Blossoms

30+ Flowers

TRYOUT PAGE

If you would like to trial your materials and colors before you start working on the designs, this page is the best place to test them.

Some of my friends put the white sheet of paper behind the page they are about to color.

You may follow the same routine.

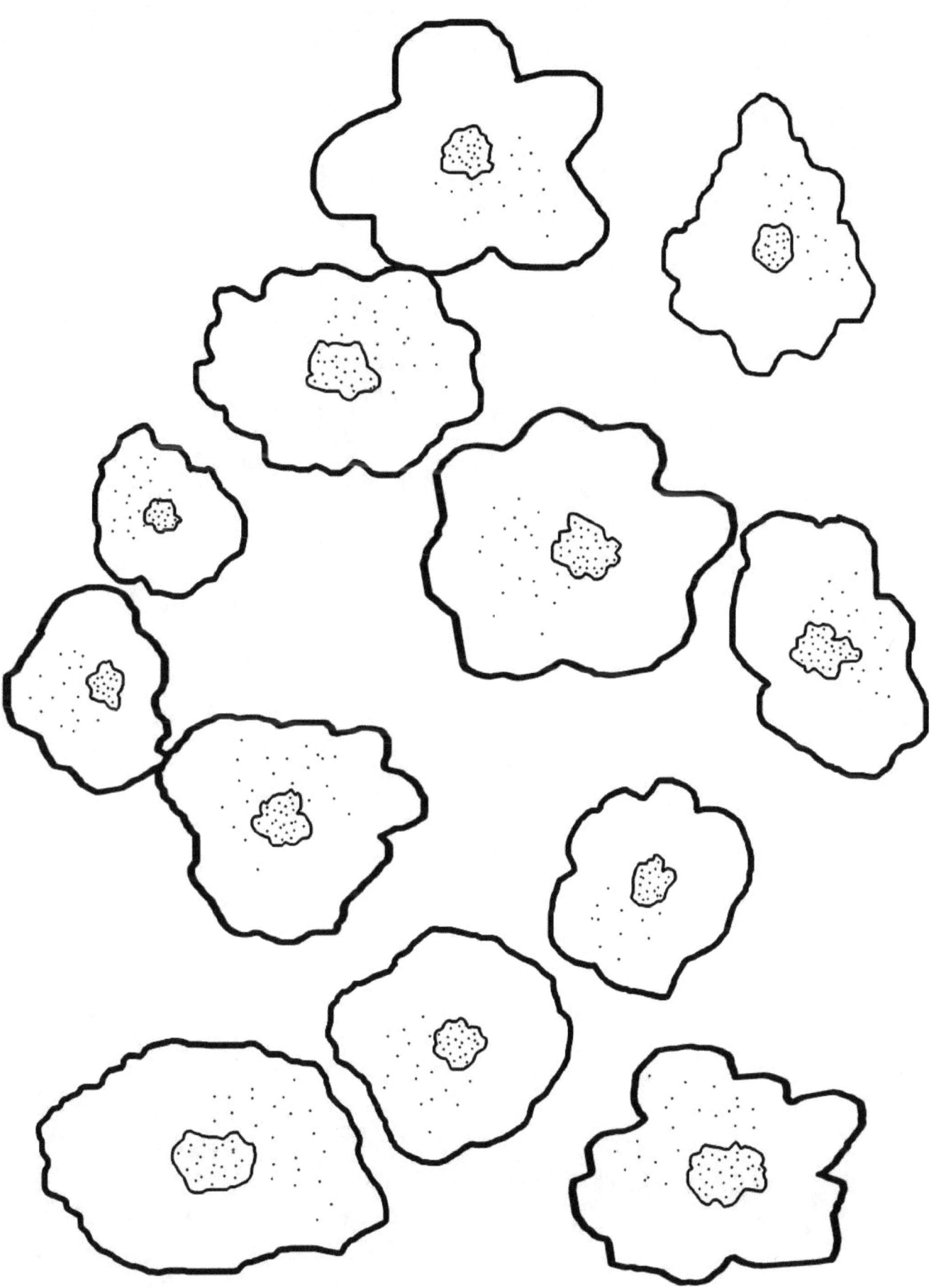

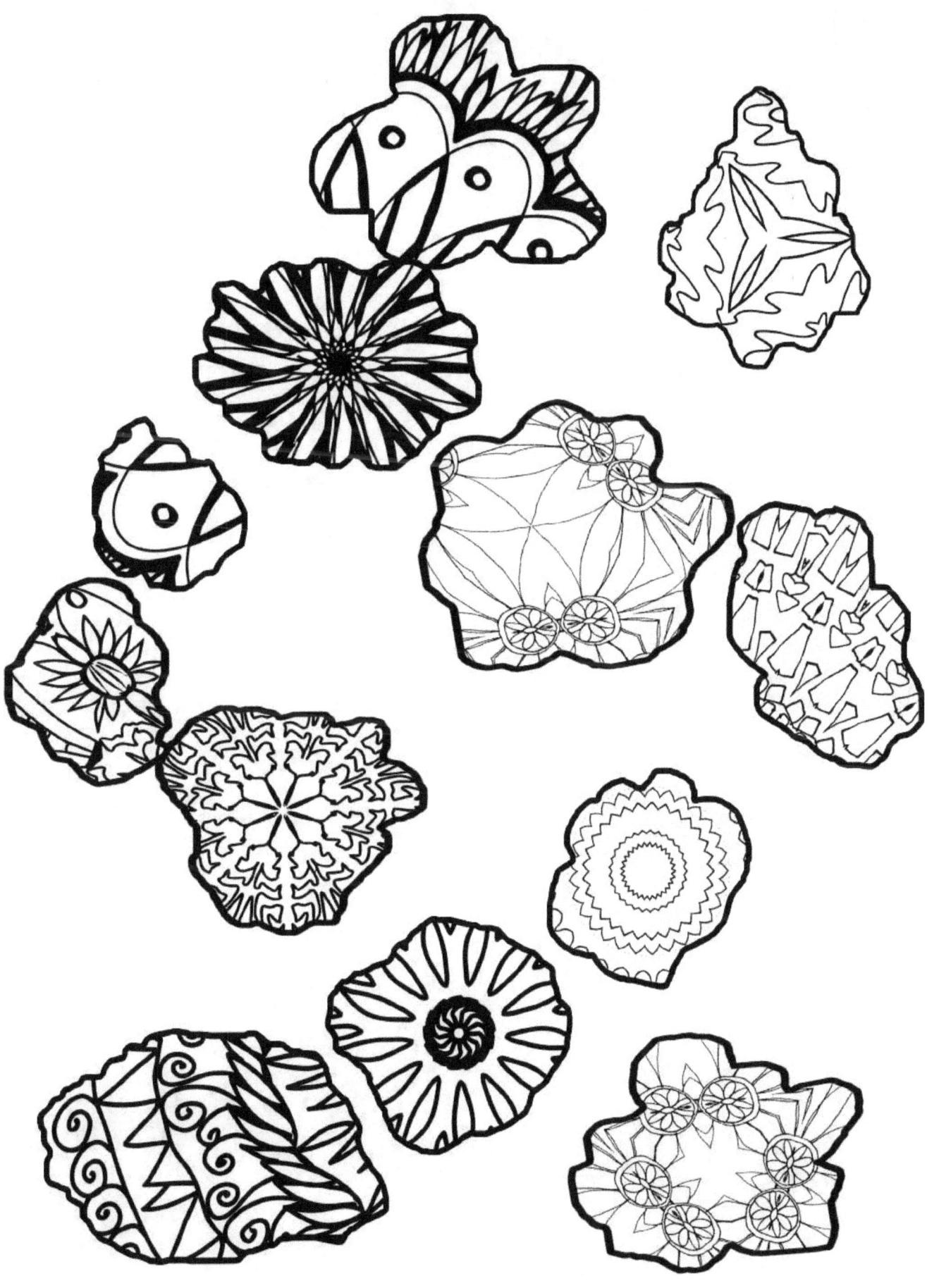

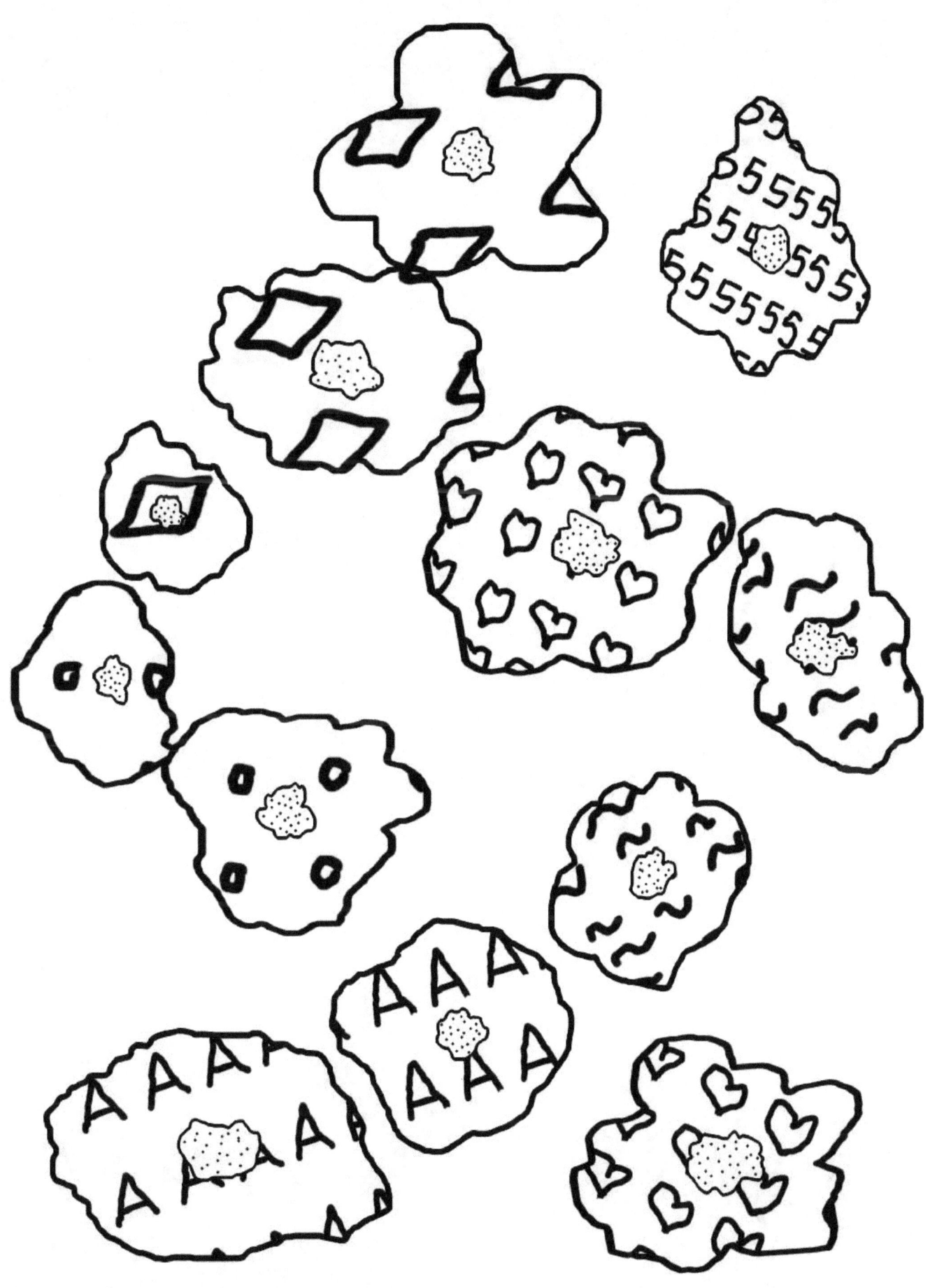

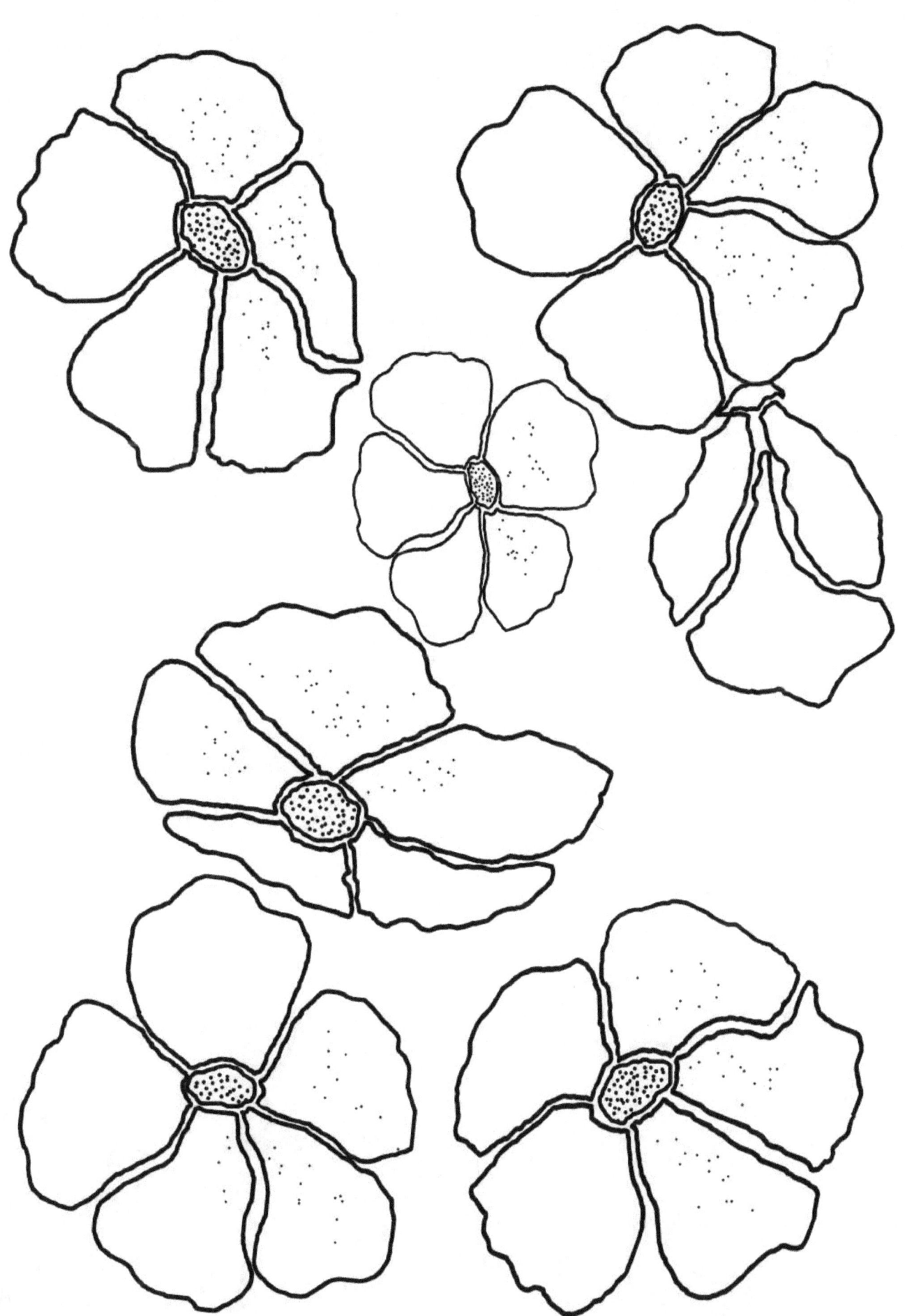

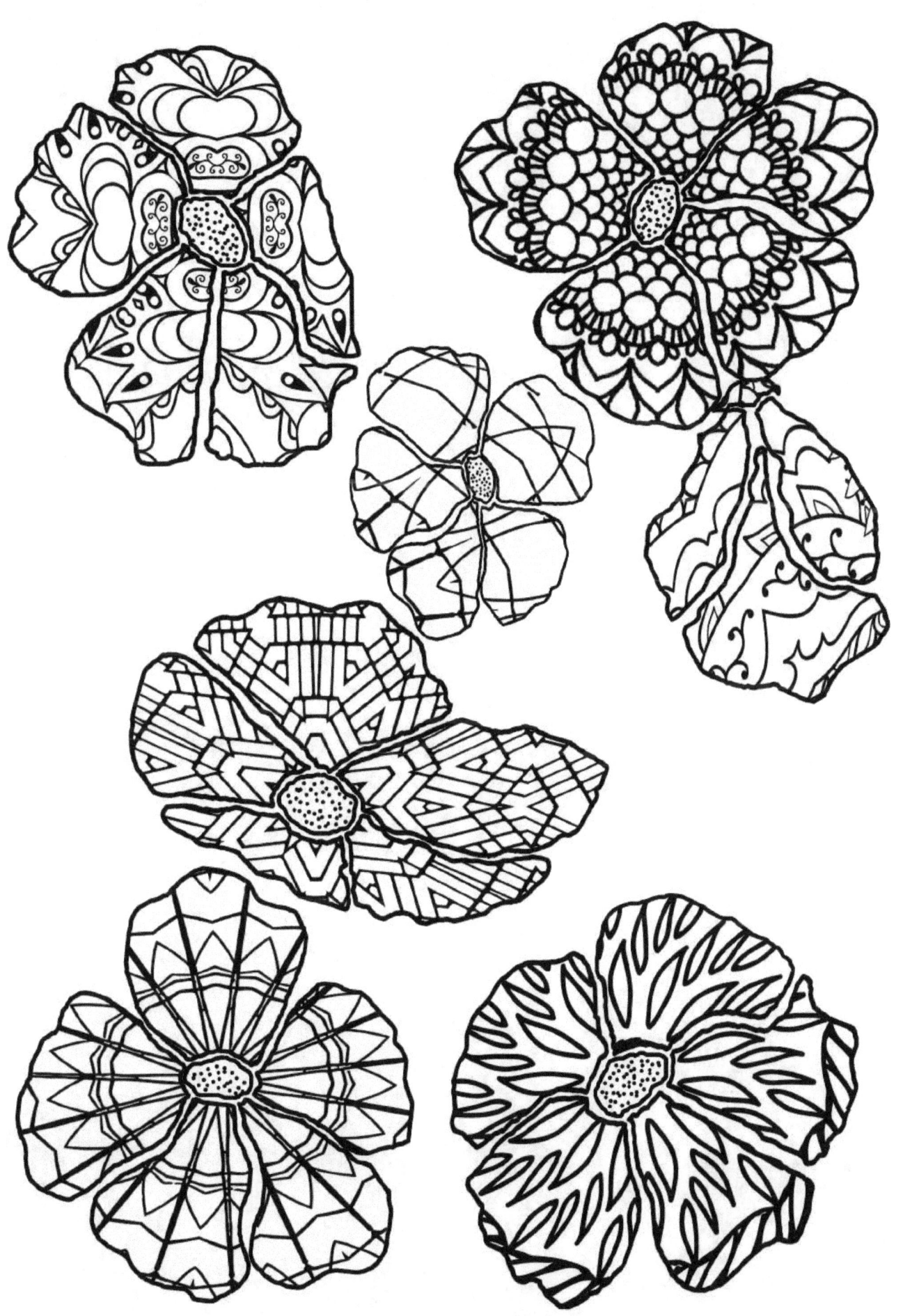

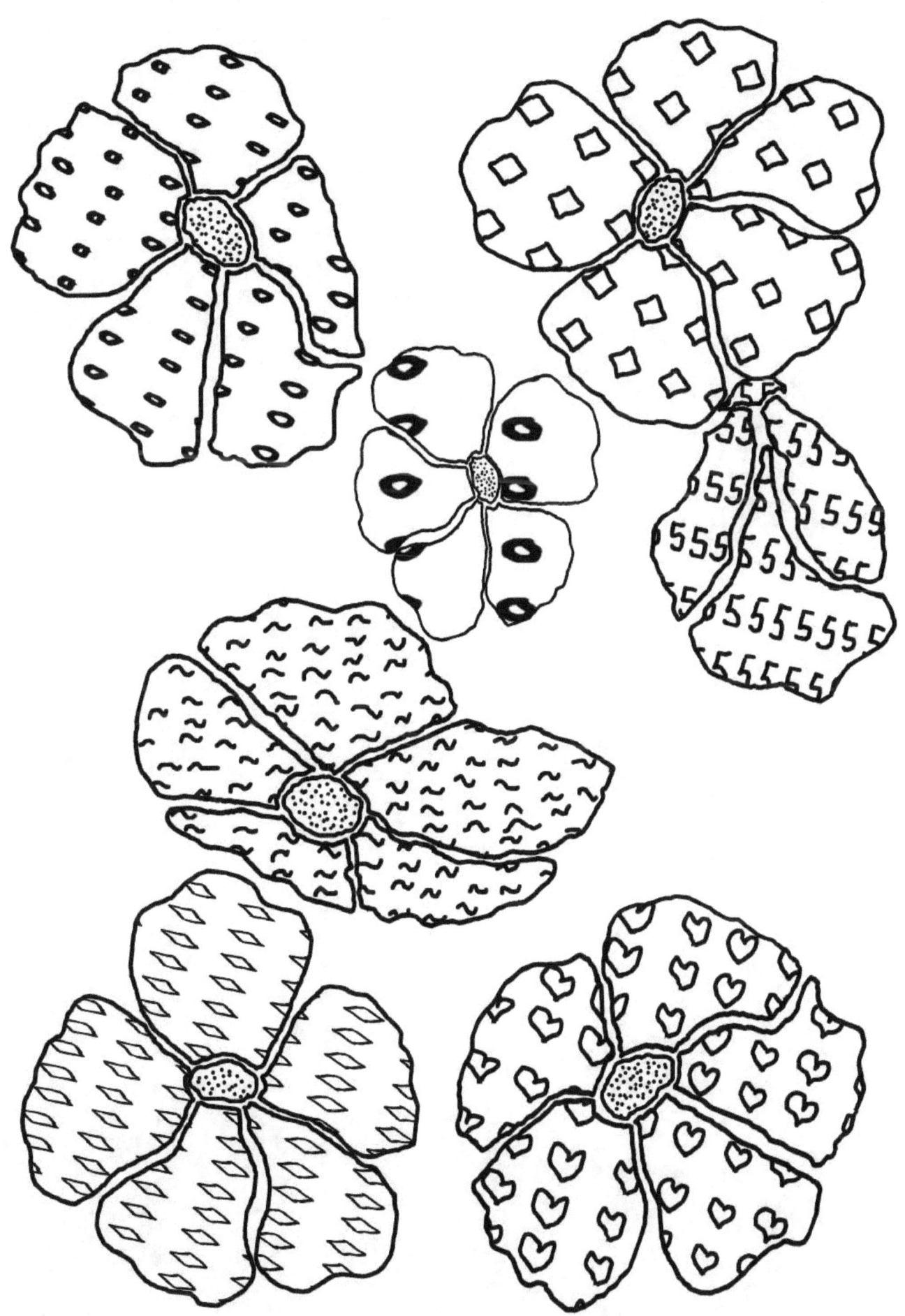

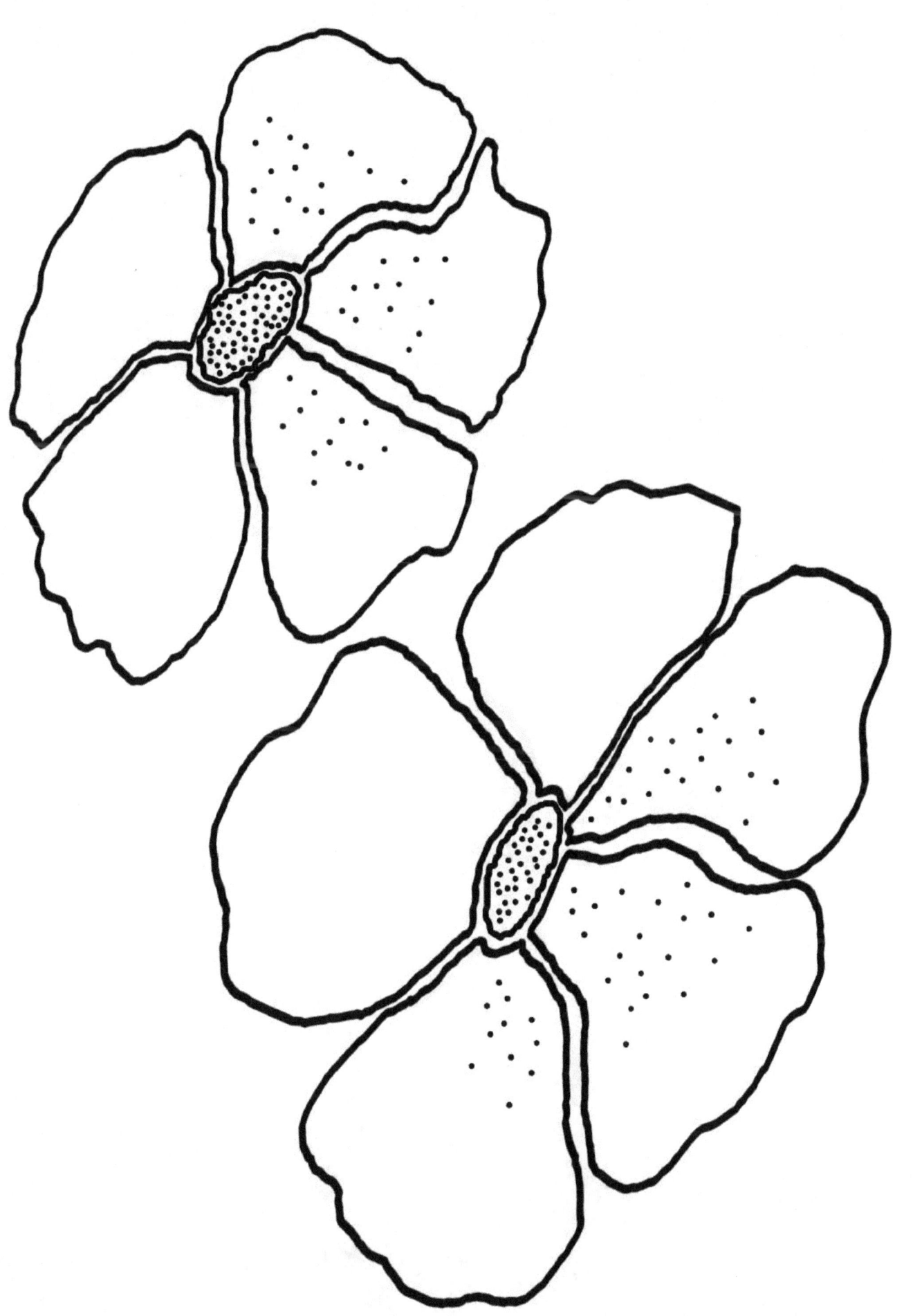

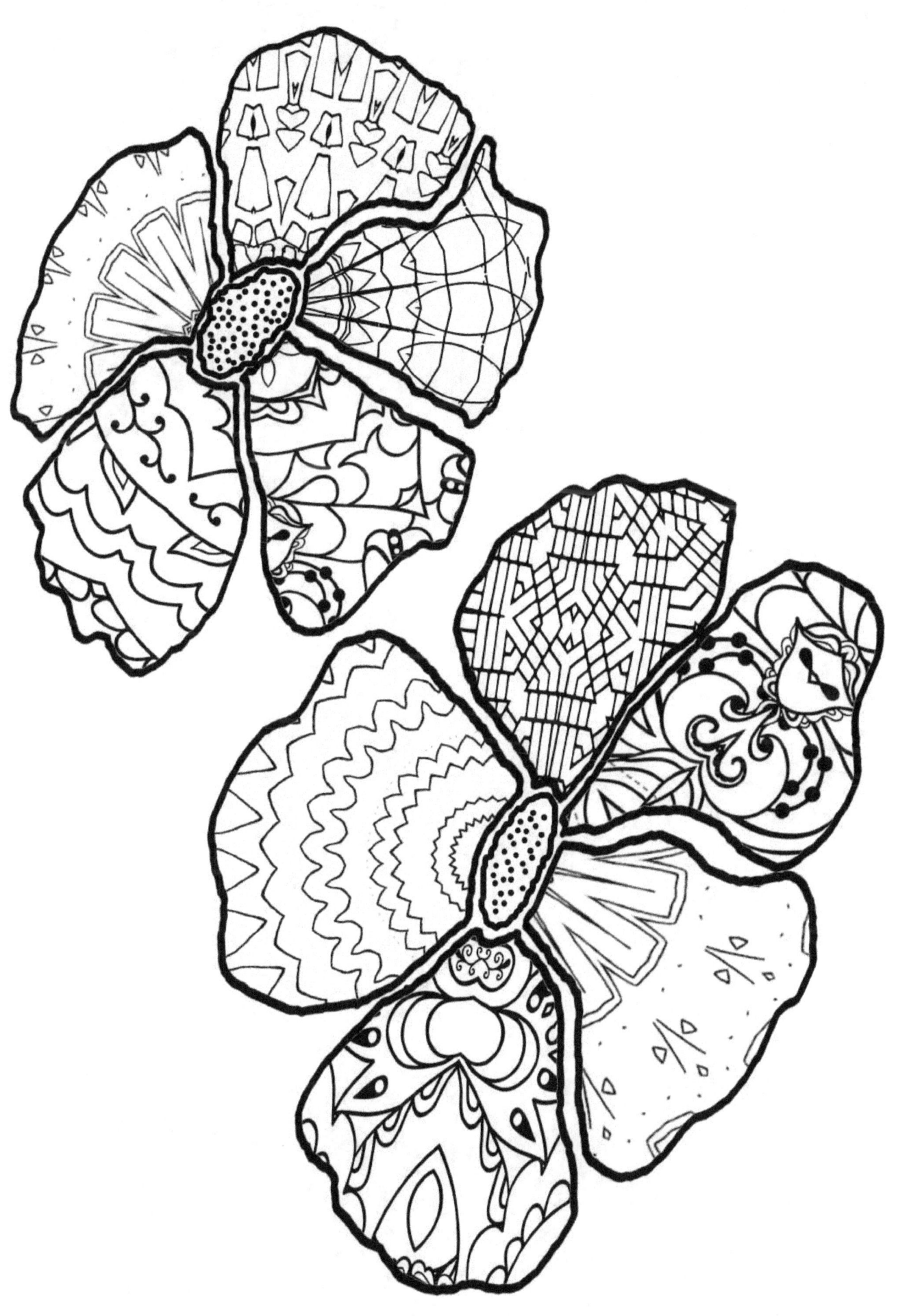

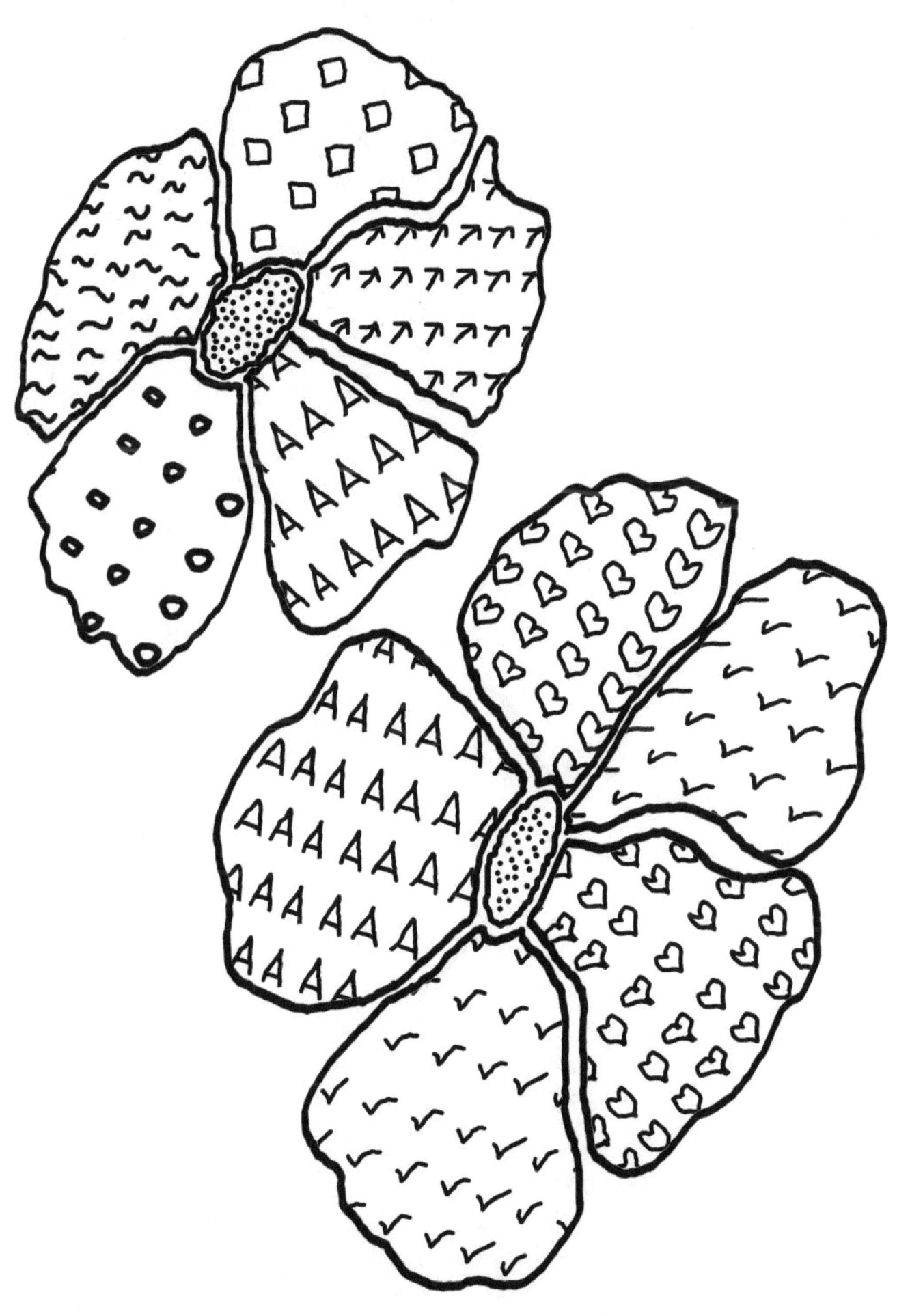

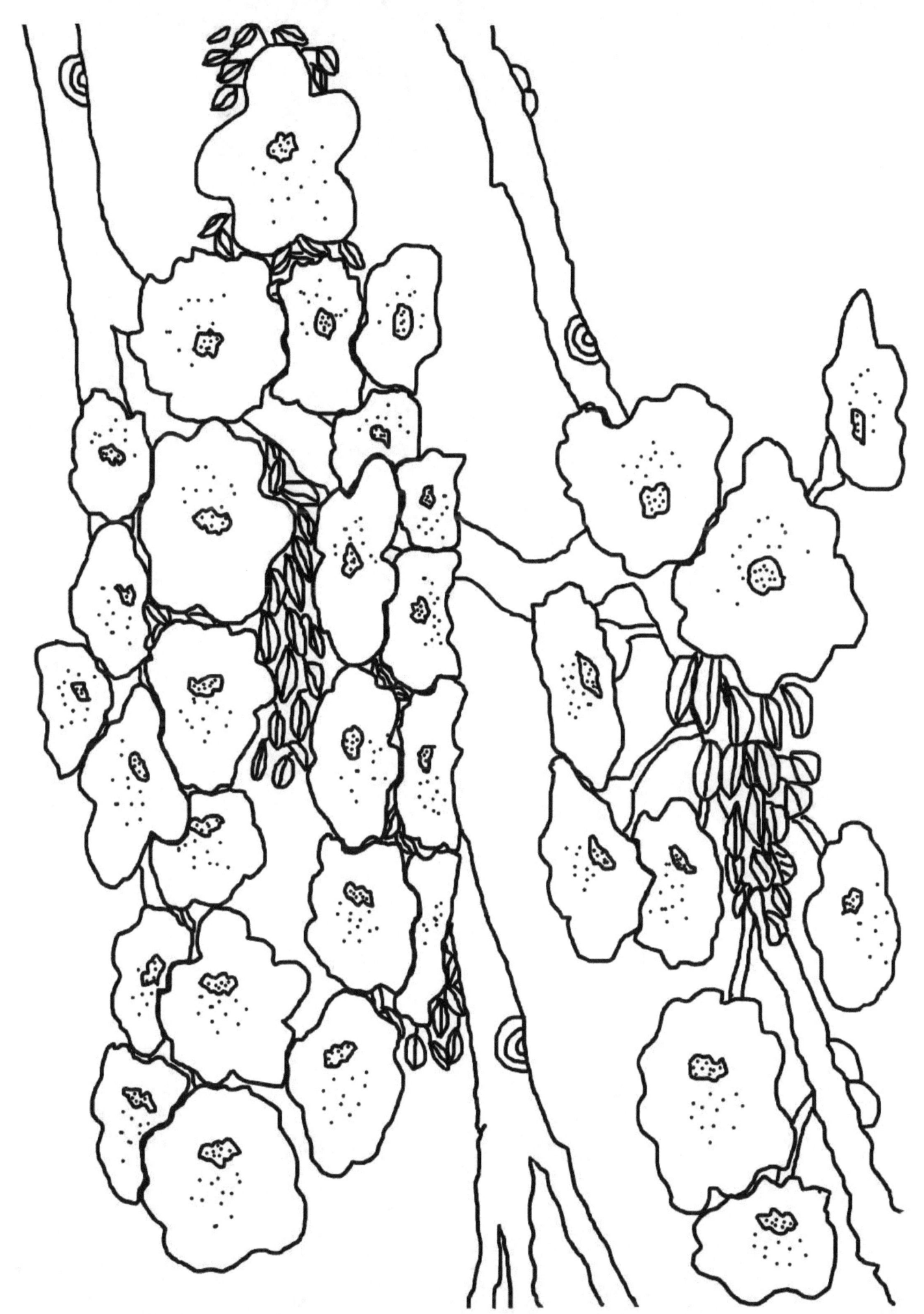

"Stress, Relaxation and Coloring Books"

Use this short book, available in the Kindle and paperback format, to enhance your relaxation practice. Dragana Dj. Jeremic, MA Psychologist and Life Coach, will lead you through stress, relaxation and coloring books.

The stress response should be short and efficient when you are in danger. But, in modern culture people are under the stress most of the time. Do you recognize the consequences of the long-term stress?

If you practice relaxation techniques daily, you'll probably gain a different mode of functioning. The relaxation response leads to a higher quality of life. Meaning, you might manifest your life priorities and feel better if you are out of the prolonged stress reaction.

Dragana dedicated every other chapter in this book to ideas of other authors. She summarizes online articles on the topics in this book. Reference section at the end of this book contains links and data, so you may study the online articles. https://amazon.com/author/draganajoy

We'll contemplate coloring books as one of the relaxation techniques. Why to relax with coloring books? What are their limitations and benefits?

"Pawsome Friends: A Community Book Project"

The book is created by Donna Kozik and 100+ contributing authors. As one of the contributing authors Dragana Dj. Jeremic wrote a short essay and a quote on the pet.

Pet lovers from around the world come together in this anthology of animal appreciation. From dogs, cats, horses, goats, birds, bunnies and pigs, these creatures are full-fledged family members to many people. Enjoy these stories about our *Pawsome Friends*!

"Fantasy Cherry Blossoms Adult Coloring Book"

This is Dragana's first coloring book. The subtitle is *Relax with the New Fantasy Coloring System*. It is available in paperback format on Amazon.

We can use the coloring book for relaxation. Another aspect is appreciating variety and change by recognizing what is similar and what is different. When you notice small changes, you may better adjust to them. The appropriate adaptation in challenging situations may be useful in life.

Dragana has drawn all the coloring pages, except for the mandala patterns that are created digitally. The one design per sheet of paper structure of the book allows you to enjoy the 28 coloring pages with the abstract quality.

Dragana's first professional degree is a museum documentarian. As a minor, she studied museology, history of art, photography, archaeology, ethnology and related subjects. Later, she took part in in-person and online courses about artistic expression.

You relax or are under stress. It is common to underestimate benefits of relaxation, but that could lead to undesirable results such as weaker immunity, health risks and lowering your levels of cognitive functioning. The prolonged stress may make worse any mood disorder like anxiety or depression, too. On the other hand, you might use Dragana's *Fantasy Cherry Blossoms Adult Coloring Book* to allow yourself to relax comfortably. It is also possible to choose from simpler to complex drawings, depending on your needs and circumstances.

Fancy Cherry Blossoms Coloring Book for Grown-Ups

Relax with Dragana's second coloring book *Fancy Cherry Blossoms Coloring Book for Grown-Ups: Enjoy the New Fantasy Coloring System (Fantasy Coloring Books)*. She designed the book to:

-Let you spend time with charming cherry blossoms in unusual ways.

-You can use imagination and remember happy events that took place in nature.

-The coloring allows you to refocus your attention from tasks and everyday obligations. It is the simple activity relaxing for your brain.

-The structure of the book allows you to recognize incremental change. What is similar in the situation? What is different here? This is fun and intellectually stimulating.

-Add dreamlike quality of the abstract coloring pages to your life.

-It is possible to choose from simpler to complex drawings, depending on your needs and circumstances.

-Let you discover the new fantasy coloring system created by Dragana Dj. Jeremic.

Easy Fantasy Cherry Blossoms Coloring Book

Yes, this coloring book is simpler than Dragana's preceding two coloring books. She listened to your requests and produced designs without the environment, just flowers in diverse shapes, quantity, patterns and positions.

If you desire to color more complex images, check Dragana's coloring books for adults. This **Easy Fantasy Cherry Blossoms Coloring Book** gives you the coloring when you've had a challenging time and would appreciate the basic coloring experience. You can also relax with your infants and/or young adults while playing with **the Easy Fantasy**.

What are the benefits of the coloring?

-Use imagination and remember happy events that took place in nature.

-The coloring allows you to refocus your attention from tasks and everyday obligations. It is the simple activity relaxing for your brain.

-Spend time with charming cherry blossoms in unusual ways.

-The structure of the book allows you to recognize incremental change. What is similar in the situation? What is different here? This is fun and intellectually stimulating.

-Add dreamlike quality of the abstract coloring pages to your life.

-It is possible to choose from simpler to complex drawings, depending on your needs and circumstances.

-Let you discover the new fantasy coloring system created by Dragana Dj. Jeremic.

I appreciate that we spent time together engaging with charming cherry blossoms. If you found this coloring book interesting and helpful, I would be grateful for your review.

Leaving a rating for Dragana's fourth coloring book will help other people find this book. You'll also support an independent author Dragana by posting your review. Writing the review gives you a chance to express yourself and be more visible in the community of readers.

Welcome to my Amazon author page, find the title *Easy Fantasy 2 Cherry Blossoms Coloring Book* and click WRITE A CUSTOMER REVIEW button. Every vote is important. You may opt for stars only. Alternatively, you may write one or several sentences to post the review.

US: https://amazon.com/author/draganajoy

Goodreads: https://www.goodreads.com/author/show/19310244.Dragana_Djordje_Jeremic

UK: https://www.amazon.co.uk/-/e/B07RN2HNBJ

Germany: https://www.amazon.de/-/e/B07RN2HNBJ

France:
https://www.amazon.fr/l/B07SN5FHP7?_encoding=UTF8&redirectedFromKindleDbs=true&ref_=pe_1805951_6402
8601&rfkd=1&shoppingPortalEnabled=true

Thank you!

You might also share the book info with your friends on social media or via email.

Kind regards,

Dragana Dj. Jeremic

www.ingramcontent.com/pod-product-compliance
Lightning Source LLC
Chambersburg PA
CBHW080854170526
45158CB00009B/2738